W9-CWZ-072

DARE TO BE A SUCCESS
Achieving Your Potential

by Dr. Robert G. Tilton

W.O.F. PUBLICATIONS
DALLAS, TEXAS

Unless otherwise indicated, all scripture quotations are from the King James Version of the Bible.

Scripture quotations marked (NIV) are from the Holy Bible, New International Version. Copyright© 1973, 1978, 1984 International Bible Society. Used by permission of Zondervan Bible Publishers.

Scripture quotations marked (AMP) are from the Amplified New Testament. Copyright© the Lockman Foundation, 1954, 1958.

Scripture quotations marked (WEY) are from the Weymouth New Testament. Copyright© Kregel Publications, 1978.

DARE TO BE A SUCCESS
Achieving Your Potential
ISBN 0-914307-61-4
Copyright© 1985 by W.O.F. Publications
First Printing May, 1985
Second Printing January, 1986

Published by W.O.F. Publications
The Publishing Division of
Word of Faith World Outreach Center
PO Box 819000, Dallas, Texas 75381-9000
Printed in the United States of America
All Rights Reserved
No Reproduction Without Permission
Illustrations by David Wilson
Cover Design by Bob Barnes

CONTENTS

INTRODUCTION

Are you a person who has sought for success, but you have never been totally fulfilled in that quest?

Have you grabbed at opportunity, only to have it slip elusively from your grasp, leading to yet another time of frustration?

Have you had a dream in your heart, but no matter how hard you tried, it evaporated, leaving that once marvelous image of success as nothing more than a whisp of your imagination?

Have you gone from disappointment to disappointment until you have almost given up all hope of succeeding?

Or have you experienced a bare minimum of success and settled for that minimum when the maximum could be right around the corner?

If your answer to any of these questions is, "Yes, Bob, you have just described me," then this book is for you.

This book is for you because it holds the only message of success that will not fail. Why? Because it is a message about God's plan for your life...and God's plan cannot fail.

God created you for a definite purpose in life—a purpose and a plan that is perfect and just for you...a plan that will fulfill some of your fondest dreams...a plan that can't help but culminate in success.

God created you to be a success! God does not make failures! It is not His nature to make failures because God never fails!

Your purpose in life is basically this: to discover and reach your maximum potential...to find and follow God's perfect plan for your life.

Get ready to launch out into the greatest adventure of your life...

Get ready to DARE TO BE A SUCCESS!

SUCCESS TRUTH:

True success is to discover and reach your maximum potential—becoming the person you were meant to be.

1

DARE TO BE A SUCCESS

Some people go through life and never really reach their full potential. But I believe that will not happen to you. Why? Because you want to reach your purpose and potential in life or you wouldn't be reading this book.

You have just taken the first step toward finding and fulfilling the perfect plan for your success!

Because you have made a decision that you want to be a success in life, you can be. Your first step toward your success was making that decision. That is why you are now on the way to fulfilling your success goal. *GOD HAS A PERFECT PLAN FOR YOUR LIFE.*

No matter how discouraged you may be with the circumstances in your life now...no matter how many disappointments you may have experienced, you *can* do some big things with what you have because God has a perfect plan for your life—a plan of success and not failure—and I am going to show you how to fit into that plan.

According to a recent Gallup Poll, 65% of all Americans believe that God has a plan for their lives. He does! And the chapters that follow will give you a step-by-step way to discover God's plan of success for your life.

You are like a seed. As with a seed, inside of you is everything good that God created you to be—your future, your destiny, your success. It is all resident on the inside of you waiting to be released into all of its fullness.

JUST WHAT IS SUCCESS?

But what really is this "success" that we are talking about?

Success for some is measured by where you live, how expensive a car you drive, your professional title, or how much money you have. While for others, success is measured in terms of health and happiness.

Recently we interviewed some people at random—people who represent all segments of society. Their responses to the question, "What does success mean to you?" were varied.

- "Success is lack of conflict in your personal life... in your marriage...with your friends."
- "I think it's when you set goals and come pretty close to realizing them."
- "Being successful is being happy...to have a good job where you can make a decent living...to have a good life."
- "It's being a good parent, a good neighbor, a good spouse...being satisfied with your life."
- "I have a lot of responsibility in my life, so to me a success is being able to perform like a responsible person."
- "I'd say success is following your dreams until they become a reality."

As many people as you ask to define success, those are the number of different answers you'll get. What are your thoughts about success? Be honest now. Do you think of success as...

...being whole and healthy physically?

...being emotionally stable and satisfied?

...being happily married or happily single?

...being famous and popular?

...being wealthy or financially secure?

There are hundreds—maybe thousands—of definitions of ''success,'' but I can assure you that there is one true, definitive definition of the word ''success,'' and in order to discover and capture your success, you need to know what it is.

SUCCESS IS BECOMING THE PERSON YOU WERE MEANT TO BE!

You were created by God for success. Your personal success does not follow someone else's pattern. Your personal success is to be what God created you to be—becoming your true self.

You will never be fulfilled until you find God's plan of success for your life because that's what you were created for. So, dare to become the person you were meant to be. And remember, any time you seek to find God's plan for your life...

1. That plan will never fail.

2. Your life will be changed for the better.

3. You will capture true success.

DARE TO BELIEVE AND CAPTURE YOUR DREAM

I challenge you to dare to read on. ''Dare'' means to aspire to your greatest aspirations...to dream your biggest dreams...and to have bold confidence that they will come to pass.

I dare you to believe that you can be a success in every area of life!

Sure, it's a challenge that will take hard work and perseverence and persistence and determination...but it's absolutely the most fulfilling, rewarding challenge you can tackle.

It's God's will for you to be fulfilled and to achieve your maximum potential. True success will come when your goal in life is to be everything that God created you to be. Let me show you, then, how to begin to unfold God's divine plan—His divine direction for your life.

SUCCESS REVIEW:

- God has a perfect plan for your life—a plan of success.
- Inside of you is everything good that God created you to be—waiting to be released.
- It's God's will for you to be fulfilled and to achieve your maximum potential.

SUCCESS TRUTH:

We can make our way prosperous relative to the agreement and application of truth in our lives.

2

DARE TO SEE THINGS AS THEY REALLY ARE

The idea of a place called heaven has always intrigued me. There are no cares in heaven...there is no sickness in heaven...there is no sorrow in heaven—there are only good things in heaven. There are only health and joy and peace in heaven.

Some recent statistics from a Gallup Poll indicate that most Americans want that same kind of heavenly life.

- 58% want to be healthy
- 49% want to be happy on their jobs
- 45% want to be happily married
- 45% want to be happy in interpersonal relationships
- others want a good education, peace of mind, and unlimited funds

What this poll really tells me is that they too want success in life. And, really, isn't that what life in heaven is all about?

HEAVEN CAN BE IN THE HERE AND NOW... NOT JUST THE HEREAFTER!

Yes, I always wanted to go to heaven, but one day I found out that heaven wanted to come to me!

I found out that God has provided all of us with the possibility of heaven on earth through His Son Jesus. That's when my life began to turn from confusion and heartache and failure. That's when I began to discover the plan of success for my life. That's when I found out that I didn't have to wait to go to heaven for all those good things I wanted. I found out that I have the ability to release the will of God as it is in heaven right here on the earth NOW. I didn't have to wait to go to heaven...heaven was possible in my life here on earth!

You may not realize it, but you were created for heaven as surely as you were created for success. And you were created for heavenly living. You were created to enjoy heaven on earth. You were not designed to be faced with strife and fear and danger and hate and all of the hideous things that go with the law of sin and death.

No, you were designed and created for the law of the spirit of life to operate on the inside of you.

There was a time in the beginning history of man when God made a place for man to dwell called Eden. It was a portion of heavenly property that was a perfect atmosphere and environment over which God gave man dominion. It was a duplication of heaven right here on earth.

But man disobeyed God, and so he lost his right to that heavenly life. He lost his ability to see things correctly. And God removed man from the Garden of Eden because of his disobedience.

But God is a just and a good God. He couldn't bear to leave man outside of the heavenly realm for which man

was created. And so He sent His Son Jesus from heaven down to earth to reveal and restore heaven to us.

I like to put it this way: A PORTION OF HEAVEN CAME TO THE EARTH THROUGH JESUS CHRIST.

The Bible tells us that Jesus prayed the same prayer that had been in my heart when He said to God, *"Thy kingdom come. Thy will be done in earth, as it is in heaven"* (Matthew 6:10).

Jesus came from heaven and was the manifestation of God the Father. When He came to earth, He literally demonstrated the will of God before mankind. It was a demonstration of heaven revealed on earth—a demonstration of healing and wholeness and peace of mind—a demonstration of success.

When Jesus said, *"I am the way, the truth, and the life"* (John 14:6), you could say that Truth came to earth as revealed through Jesus. The truth about God...the truth about heaven...and the truth about the will of God.

That's why we need to turn our attention to the one book that tells us the truth about God's will for our life—The Bible.

WE CAN TRUST ONLY IN TRUTH

Here's a success truth you can count on:

We make our own way prosperous relative to the application of the truth and the wisdom of God in our lives.

In other words...

Our ability to prosper depends upon the amount of truth and wisdom that comes from God which we know and exercise and apply to our lives.

Since the Bible tells us that *all* scripture is given to us by the inspiration and direction of God Himself (II Timothy 3:16), then it is *imperative* that we know what the Bible says. The Bible is profitable for instructions in how to deal wisely in all the affairs of life. So it is *vital* that we know what the Bible says if we want to operate our lives in Godly wisdom...if we want to be successful.

THE BIBLE IS THE ORIGINAL SUCCESS BOOK!

There's a passage in the Bible in which God is quoted as saying, *"My people are destroyed for lack of knowledge"* (Hosea 4:6).

Knowledge is information, and the right kind of information gives us the ability to see things correctly and gets us in agreement with truth.

You were designed to operate wisely in all of the affairs of life. You were designed to judge things correctly—to call it and tell it like it really is. You were designed to see things clearly and correctly and accurately. And if you can't see things correctly, you do not know how to judge between that which is really right and that which is really wrong.

When you have Godly wisdom...

- You can tell the difference between a lie and the truth...

- You can tell the difference between darkness and light...

- You can tell the difference between evil and good...

- You can tell the difference between that which is hellish and that which is heavenly...

- You can tell the difference between failure and SUCCESS!

LOOK AGAIN!

We can't always trust in the things which we see or hear, or even in the way that we feel. But we can go to the source of all life—we can go to the greatest book of instructions on how to live life to the fullest—The Bible.

The Bible is not just a series of fables or fancy words. It is literally *the* source book to lay the unshakable foundation that will build your life on a solid rock.

This is why the Bible admonishes us to meditate on its words "day and night," because you will literally be taking in heavenly information. You are opening up the eyes of your understanding so that you will know how to bring heaven into your life on earth. You are receiving information that will enable you to conquer life's problems.

Let me ask you some questions, and I want you to be honest with yourself when you reply.

- Have you ever made a mistake?

- Have you ever had insurmountable problems?

- Have you ever been confused and frightened?

- Have you ever wondered what to do?

Well, I have good news for you!

THE WILL OF GOD IS THAT YOU KNOW
WHAT TO DO IN *EVERY* SITUATION.

The problem is that we become blinded by our circumstances and feelings. We need to have our eyes opened to the truth. And I mean the truth as it *really* is, not as it appears to be.

The words which are in the Bible and the truth they contain have life and power behind them. They contain truth that is powerful enough to bring a release of inspiration...powerful enough to move the mountains in your life that are blocking your path to God's perfect plan.

Let's look now at a verse from the Bible that contains some potent success keys:

"This book of the law shall not depart out of thy mouth; but thou shalt meditate therein day and night, that thou mayest observe to do according to all that is written therein: for then thou shalt make thy way prosperous, and then thou shalt have good success" Joshua 1:8.

Now let's examine this verse of scripture in detail.

1. *"This book of the **law**..."*
   (Truth, information, and the quality of being in agreement with reality or fact)

2. *"...Shall not depart out of thy **mouth**..."*
   (Speak the truth as it is written in the Bible)

3. *"...But thou shalt **meditate** therein..."*
   (Think seriously about it, study, ponder, and reflect upon it)

4. *"...Day and night..."*
   (All the time, continuously)

5. *"...That thou mayest observe to **do** according to **all** that is written therein..."*
   (Be obedient to act upon it, follow the direction it gives, abide by its laws)

6. *"...For then thou shalt make thy way **prosperous**..."*
(All your needs will be supplied, you will have plenty, abundance will be your reward)

7. *"...And then thou shalt have good **success**."*
(You will be the person you were meant to be, you will reach maximum potential in every area of life, and you will be fulfilled)

Did you notice that this verse of scripture says that YOU must do these specific things, and *then* God will supply the reward or blessing that is a result of your actions? That means that we have OUR part to play and God has HIS part. You have to do all that it says to do. You have to put it to work in your life. Your actions have to come in line, or agreement, with truth. This is how we begin to build our strong foundation for right living and success—upon the bedrock of truth.

It's like this:
When you get your believing right...
when you get your thinking right...
when you get your speaking right...
and when you get your actions right...
THEN YOU WILL GET YOUR RECEIVING RIGHT!

It's exciting to think that this Bible, which for years I used to think was just a dusty old history book and not relative to the problems I was facing in life, is now my lifeline to victorious living! Through its words of life and power I learned how to break every curse of cause and effect through the bad things that try to come against me. And by putting its words to work in my life, I have learned how to deal wisely in all circumstances.

Why? Because...
WE MAKE OUR WAY PROSPEROUS RELATIVE TO THE AGREEMENT AND APPLICATION OF TRUTH IN OUR LIVES.

It begins with God's Word—the Bible—which is the "heavenly prescription" for right-living, right-thinking, and right-action. When you feed it into your mind, then it settles in your heart and becomes a SUCCESSFUL WAY OF LIFE!

SUCCESS REVIEW:

- Heaven can be in the here and now...not just the hereafter.
- You were designed and created for the law of the spirit of life to operate on the inside of you.
- Jesus was the demonstration of the will of God for our lives—heaven revealed on earth in the form of healing, wholeness, peace of mind, and success.
- Our ability to prosper depends upon the amount of God's truth and wisdom that we know, exercise, and apply to our lives. The Bible is the source book of that truth—the key to our success in life.

SUCCESS TRUTH:

When we change our thinking to thoughts of the good and acceptable and perfect will of God, our whole life can be transformed with that same goodness and perfection.

3

DARE TO UTILIZE THE POWER OF A HARNESSED MIND

Most people don't know how to control their thinking. They allow all kinds of negative thoughts to enter their minds. Eventually those thoughts make destructive inroads, thoughts that begin to rule and destroy their lives.

These kind of thoughts are not controlled by truth—truth, as we learned in the previous chapter, which comes from God for our good.

Let me give you an example. Possibly you have heard of the alarming statistics about the frequency of teenage suicides that have come like a plague against our young people. Recently within a short time frame there were six teenage suicides in one small town of only twenty-two thousand people. Now, that's an awfully high percentage of the population to take their lives. It is an alarming statistic but, unfortunately, a situation that is happening with more and more frequency.

Suicide is an extreme example of the result of an uncontrolled, or unharnessed mind.

Those young people didn't know how to control their thinking and harness their minds with the power of truth. So when thoughts of destruction assailed their thoughts, they just agreed with them and ultimately acted on them.

"Yes, it's true that no one loves me—no one cares." Or, "There is no answer to my problem—no way out." Or, "I might as well give up."

No one taught them that there is a plan of success for each of our lives. They didn't know that they were listening to lies and not harnessing their minds with the bridle of truth that would have given them life instead of death.

I like to use the terms "harness" and "bridle" in connection with this subject of your mind because they mean "anything that controls or restrains; used for guidance." You see, it's important to learn to harness your mind—to control and restrain the thoughts that try to enter and hurt you.

The truth as God conveys it is the only thing that we must allow to dominate and guide our lives.

WATCH OUT FOR THOSE BIRDS OF PREY

I like the way someone once put it. It's humorous, but it makes a very serious point.

"A bird can fly over," he said, "but you don't have to let it build a nest on your head."

This means that a thought may pass across your mind, but you can choose whether or not to dwell on it, and ultimately act on it. If the thought is negative and destructive, it can lead you on the path to failure instead of on the success path that God planned for you.

A mind left to its own devices will just continually wander aimlessly. Conversely, there is tremendous power for good when you harness your thinking and bring it under the bridle of truth.

YOU HAVE THE CAPACITY FOR BRILLIANCE

Upon the death of Albert Einstein, the genius physicist who formulated the theory of relativity, scientists analyzed his brain. They discovered that he had used approximately 10% of his thinking capacity.

The average person uses somewhere between 6% and 8% of his mind's unlimited capacity.

Just think, it took only a little bit of extra effort on the part of Einstein—a tiny bit more extra mental effort—to produce his brilliant theories. Things that no one else had ever thought about before came from his mind.

Then, imagine what you could accomplish with a mind harnessed by good thoughts...thoughts inspired by God and His infinite supply of wisdom.

Just as He did with Einstein, God created you with a brain and a mind that has the ability to think and choose its thoughts. And he enabled your mind to exercise will power. He created your mind for accomplishment, success, and brilliance.

God didn't make Einstein better than He made you. It's just that he was a man who learned how to bridle and take command of his thoughts. He learned the value of accepting some thoughts and rejecting others.

RETENTION SPAN STATISTICS

It has been determined that when people learn something, they forget far more than they retain.

- Within 24 hours you forget 25%
- Within 48 hours you forget 50%
- Within 4 days you forget 80%
- Within 16 days you forget 98%

And when you listen to someone speak, it is said that you hear only about 50% of the entire message.

Your attention wanders. You are interrupted by distractions. You suddenly remember something that seems more important than what you are now hearing. All kinds of things happen to keep you from the words which are trying to get your attention, and so you end up hearing only half of what is being said, and retaining far less than what you hear.

DON'T OPERATE WITHOUT TRANSMITTING POWER

When you stop to think about it, it is incredible to realize how little of our created ability to think and create we actually utilize, how few of our created success abilities we actually profit from.

Most of the time our mind is idle. It is there, it's alive, but it's going in no particular, or bridled, direction. It doesn't have a destination, a plan or a purpose. Our thoughts move aimlessly. In other words, our mind is operating without transmitting power!

Most of the time our mind is there, but it is really not doing anything beneficial, such as when apathy has set in. What a tragic waste of our God-given human potential.

AIMLESS WANDERING IS INEFFECTIVE

An unharnessed mind is why roughly 95% of the people in the world move aimlessly through life without purpose or direction. These people are unproductive and ineffective, and they contribute little or nothing to the society in which they live. If they did have direction and purpose and a harnessed mind, those same 95% could grow to become powerful and successful in every area of their lives. But instead they float through life idly, giving little if any value to either themselves or others.

The Bible says it like this:

"...An idle soul shall suffer hunger" (Proverbs 19:15). Let me break that down for you so that you will see what it conveys about our subject of a harnessed mind.

First, the word "idle" in this Bible verse means to move or wander aimlessly. You've heard references to an idle mind being the devil's playground. That's because idle minds are open to taking in and believing false information—information which is ultimately harmful to us. A mind that is idle is non-engaged, unbridled, and non-productive.

Next, the word "hunger" means to go without that which is essential for health, productivity, and even life itself. Your brain was designed to be fed with good thoughts and good ideas which would then produce good results. But a brain that "hungers" can't produce much at all.

YOU NEED TO REACH YOUR DESTINED DESTINATION

Remember, we learned that God created everyone with a single purpose in life—to reach his or her maximum potential and to be everything that God created each of us to be. To say it another way, that also means reaching your destined destination!

God gave each of us a brain through which His purposes in us could be fulfilled. But it is up to us to protect and feed and nourish that brain properly. Truth must be accepted and lies rejected.

This is how you can bring your mind in subjection to God's plan and purpose for your life. This keeps you established in hope and defeats discouragement that limits your progress.

STABILITY LEADS TO SUCCESS

Hope, according to the Bible, is an anchor to your soul (Hebrews 6:19). That means that establishing a purpose or a goal in your life stabilizes your thinking. Stability keeps you directed firmly on the path of success.

The reason that hope is so healthy for our minds (which is what your soul is), is that you were created by God to have a purpose in life...a direction...a plan...or a goal. You aren't satisfied or fulfilled until you are walking in that plan.

Perhaps you have suffered from mental depression that has assailed your mind and inhibited your hope. Perhaps you have even contemplated suicide like the young people I told you about.

If so, it is because you have not learned how to harness your thinking with the Word of God...with God's ideas... with God's wisdom...with God's hope...with God's plan for your life.

HOW TO HARNESS YOUR THINKING

In order to operate in God's plan for your life...

- You must build your life on the Word of God.
- You must build your marriage on the Word of God.
- You must build your business affairs on the Word of God.
- You must build your finances on the Word of God.
- You must build your hope on the Word of God.

The bottom line is this: All that you do must be directed and guided by God through His instructions for successful living as outlined in the Bible.

The Bible can rightly be called, "God's Success Manual." The Bible can activate all your unused brain cells. Just imagine what you can accomplish by using your unused 90-95% brain power!

YOUR FEELINGS MAY BE LYING TO YOU

Think of your mind like a castle. You are like a king who lives in a castle. You have a moat around your castle with a drawbridge by which you control who comes into or out of your castle. By pulling the bridge up or down, you can let into your life whatever you want to. And you can keep out whatever you want to. You are the king of your castle, so you have the power of choice.

If you are trusting in how you feel...

If you are trusting in how things look...

If you are trusting in what you have or don't have...

If you are trusting in these things which motivate your feelings, then you will fail.

But if you are trusting in what God says about your situation, you will succeed.

If you want to have heaven on earth—if you want to have success in all that you do—then YOU have to harness your mind by "pulling up the drawbridge" at the right time to keep out wrong thoughts. Conversely, you have to "let down the drawbridge" to the Word of God.

REPLACE THE IMPOSSIBLE WITH THE POSSIBLE

Your normal human mind falls so far short of what God will reveal to you, if you let Him. When you begin to read the over 7,000 promises of God in the Bible and see how big His plans are for you, it will, as the kids say, "blow your mind"! That's why you can't be conformed to this world, but must be conformed to God's world instead.

Your mind needs to be reconditioned by God's thoughts so that you can see the possible in place of the impossible.

THE PIKE AND THE MINNOWS

Let me tell you a story which will illustrate what I am saying. It involves a scientific experiment by a group of researchers studying the conditioning process.

They got an aquarium in which they placed many minnows and a large pike. Pike is a game fish that is normally found in fresh water, and it thrives on minnow dinners. Naturally, the pike just gobbled up those little minnows and had a feast for himself.

Then the scientists put a pane of glass across the middle of the aquarium so that the new minnows they added were on one side of the glass, and the pike was contained on the other side. The glass partition remained in place for several weeks.

The pike would run up to the glass trying to get at the minnows, but he'd just hit his head, getting nowhere. He'd see the minnows, but he couldn't get to them.

Then one day the scientists pulled out the glass. The pike swam freely all around the minnows, but he didn't eat even one of them. Why? Because by this time, he had been conditioned by the presence of the glass and its limitations, so he just assumed he couldn't eat minnows anymore.

Eventually the pike died of starvation, circled and surrounded by delicious little minnows, because he had been conditioned to believe that he could no longer eat them.

It is the same way with us...

- We become conditioned to lack...
- We become conditioned to face "insurmountable" problems...
- We become conditioned to sickness...
- We become conditioned to failure.

This is the result of coming under the influence of the world of man instead of the world of God. It's like the pike. If he had stopped going by how things looked, or how he thought they looked, then he could have eaten a batch of delicious minnows and lived to eat more. Instead, he died of starvation because he refused to change his thinking!

RENEW YOUR MIND WITH GOD'S THINKING

Our minds can be released to new accomplishments, new life, and new success if we renew our minds with God's thinking.

When we change our thinking to those things which are the good and acceptable and perfect will of God, our whole lives can be transformed with that same goodness and perfection.

Your mind can be renewed to bring forth the will of God as it is in heaven down into your life on earth.

I want you to see this and get your thinking changed. I want you to be able to know how to harness your mind with the truth instead of the lies you have been believing. I want you to come out from under the influence of the lack, and strife, and hurt, and heartaches of this world. I want you to be free from poverty and failure. I want you to be free from lies and limitations.

YOU CAN LET TRUTH PREVAIL IN YOUR LIFE

But you have a responsibility to do something. Your responsibility is to push back the gates of hell that have prevailed against your mind. Your responsibility is to choose the perfect will of God...the perfect thoughts of

God...the truth of God.

- Truth prevails over sickness.
- Truth prevails over disease.
- Truth prevails over discouragement.
- Truth prevails over doubts.
- Truth prevails over inferiority.
- Truth prevails over failure.

Truth is telling you now that you have the maximum potential of seeing your fondest dreams come true...the potential of reaching your highest goals.

This is because God can do for you what is far above what you could ever ask or think.

So don't waste another minute in the ultimate achieving of your success. *Right now* determine to begin harnessing your thoughts and make God's perfect choices for your life.

SUCCESS REVIEW:

- The truth as God conveys it in the Bible is the only thing that we must allow to dominate and guide our lives.
- A thought may pass across your mind, but you can choose whether to dwell and ultimately act on it. If the thought is negative and destructive, it can lead to failure instead of success.
- When we change our thinking to thoughts of the good and acceptable and perfect will of God, our whole life can be transformed with that same goodness and perfection.
- When your mind is reconditioned by God's thoughts, you can see the possible in place of the impossible.

SUCCESS TRUTH:

Ask God for what you want, or you're going to have to settle for what you get.

4

DARE TO EXERCISE YOUR POWER OF CHOICE

Whether you realize it or not, *you* have the power of choice, the power to choose to make your life a failure or a success.

You have the power to choose blessings or cursings...life or death.

You have the power to choose your direction and your destiny.

Now *that's* a *lot* of *power!*

You might say, "Bob, I thought that whatever will be will be."

No, that's a lie you've been believing which has robbed you of your power to choose success.

You might say, "Bob, I always thought some people were lucky and some just weren't."

No, there's no such thing as luck. It's called being blessed. And it comes from choosing to follow God's success plan, whether you realize you are following it or not.

TAKE POSSESSION OF YOUR PROMISED LAND

God has prepared a "promised land" for you, just as He did for the children of Israel from the Old Testament story. God wanted to bless them just the way He wants to bless you, but they had to choose to receive that blessing. They had to choose to enter their promised land. Just as yours is, it was a land prepared for their prosperity and success in life.

According to the Bible story, there were the children of Israel, having gone through years of wandering through the wilderness, and they were finally camped on the Jordan River overlooking the land which God had promised to give them. All they had to do was walk on into it.

But because the land was strange to them, they decided to send twelve men to investigate this unknown land to make sure it was safe to enter. Ten of the men came back saying the land was too dangerous. Fear was keeping them from believing God.

But two of the men came back and said, "Sure, the land has some hazards, but God gave it to us, so we can handle it. With God on our side, we can overcome anything." The fear of ten kept the children of Israel bound for 40 years before they went in and took their land.

You have the same power of choice in life that they did. You can let fear keep you from your "promised land," or you can decide to move ahead and possess it.

God gives *us* the choice between receiving His blessings or letting them go unclaimed.

YOU DECIDE AND DECREE

Here's another Bible verse that emphasizes this point.

"Thou shalt also decree a thing, and it shall be established unto thee: and the light shall shine upon thy ways" (Job 22:28).

In other words, when you make the right decision, you release God's best into your life—you literally release

heaven into the earth on your behalf. You have the power to release the will of God for your benefit so that "darkness" can be replaced by "light."

You have the power to decide and decree your own success! Many people are waiting for opportunity to knock, as the old saying goes. But this verse tells us that...

You don't wait for the opportunity to knock—you do the knocking!

You don't have to stay in the condition you're in right now. Whatever level you're at, you can always grow and aspire to new and bigger dreams.

YOU do the knocking...

YOU do the seeking...

YOU do the asking...

...THE CHOICE IS YOURS!

Ask God for what you want, or you're going to have to settle for what you get!

It's *not* whatever will be will be.

It's *not* a matter of waiting for opportunity to knock.

It's *not* luck.

It's *not* signs you must follow.

Signs are to follow you instead of you following signs!

ASK FOR GOD'S BEST

When you begin to act upon the more than 7,000 promises God has made to those who love and obey Him, those 7,000 "seeds" begin to be harvested in your life. And if you sow daily, you will reap daily. It's the law of cause and effect. Whatever you sow, that's what you'll reap. For every action, there is a reaction.

Ask God for what you want, or you're going to have to settle for what you get! Lay hold of the promises of God, and you'll get the best.

Begin to see that you have the power of choice between good and evil. Decide and decree the best that God has for you, and you will be amazed at how your life will begin to change.

Dare to be a success. Do something about your life instead of sitting there and passively floating downstream. Any old dead fish can float downstream. It takes a live one to make a choice to go against the current—to make a choice to exert the power to move toward a better life.

IT'S TIME FOR A HEART CHECKUP

There's a verse in the Book of Proverbs, Chapter 23, verse 7, which contains a special truth. It tells us that as a person thinks in the depths of his heart, that's the way he really is.

I looked up the key words ''think'' and ''heart'' in the original Hebrew translation.

- *Think* means, ''as he reasons, as he calculates, as he discerns, as he judges.'' Or...AS HE CHOOSES WISELY.
- *Heart* means, ''soul, area of the will, mind, intellect.'' Or...THE POWER OF CHOICE.

So, as a person thinks, as a person decides, as a person judges in the area of his will...so is he...

so is his health...

so is his marriage...

so is his financial situation...

so is every area of his life!

How you think and how you judge determines what you allow to go out from you, and what you allow to come into your life. *You* have the power of choice. *Your* will decides. *You* reason and you choose according to the information that you have gathered. If the information you have gathered is not truth, then you are going to decide and judge things the wrong way. Your choice will be a wise choice if it is based upon the truth of God's Word. Why? Because, as we learned, anything else can't be depended upon to be truth because things aren't always the way they seem to be.

Any time you step out of the way things actually are, you open yourself wide to the deceptions and lies of the devil. Adam and Eve stepped out of the way of ''things as they actually were'' when they listened to the devil in the Garden of Eden instead of listening to God. You could say that by doing this they short-circuited their system. They came crosswise with the truth and lost their ''promised land.''

WHAT IS A LIE?

A lie is...

- a deception
- something that misleads
- something that directs the wrong way
- an illusion
- incorrect or faulty vision
- a misrepresentation of the truth

Adam and Eve were blinded to the truth when the devil in the guise of a serpent lied to them. By disobeying God, they not only lost their right to live in the perfect land of the Garden of Eden, but they also died spiritually.

Because of what Adam and Eve did to disobey God and receive His punishment, mankind was affected. Mankind then inherited this spiritual separation. You and I inherited this spiritual separation—this inability to see things as they actually are.

THERE *IS* A WAY OUT OF OUR SPIRITUAL DEATH

But God is a just and merciful God, and He made provision for man to be redeemed from his spiritual condition. He gave us a choice when God sent His son Jesus for our redemption. Romans 5:17 puts it this way:

"For if by one man's offence death reigned by one; much more they which receive abundance of grace and of the gift of righteousness shall reign in life by one, Jesus Christ."

Spiritually speaking, we came under the dominion of lies and could not see actuality and truth. But now because of the gift of righteousness that Jesus offers us, we have the choice of being restored back into the success position that we were supposed to have when God created man in the Garden of Eden. Now, through Jesus, we can bring heaven down into our life here on earth!

Whether we make the choice to do that or not is up to us. God has given us the power of choice. It is up to us to exercise it for our good.

TRUTH HAS COME TO SET US FREE

The truth has come in the person of Jesus. The will of God as it is in heaven has come in Jesus to set humanity—you and me—free from failure—free to receive success.

When I found out that it was the will of God for me to be able to pay my bills and have some money left over, I got excited.

When I found out that it was the will of God for my body to be physically well, I got excited.

When I found out that it was the will of God for me to be successful in *every* area of my life, I got excited.

I found out I don't have to wait until I get to heaven to pay my bills...have healing for my body...have success. I found out that heaven has already come to earth for me...and that I have the power to release it into my life by an action of choice.

You're not limited by your senses to the quality of life that God has for you. You are only limited by your decision to make the wrong or right choices.

YOU HAVE BEEN REDEEMED TO BE A SUCCESS

I know a man who had a desire to retire early from his job. He had that dream and decided to act on it even though it looked foolhardy to some people. But this man knew that God had given him a choice in life, and so this man had the courage to follow his dream.

He took his life savings, and he and his wife bought a run-down laundromat at a bargain price. He worked around the clock to fix it up and put it in operable condition.

When that first laundromat was opened and running successfully he bought another one, then another one. Pretty soon he had five of them in successful operation. So he went out and bought a whole shopping center.

Why is this man prosperous and successful? Because he exercised his power of choice and believed God's Word. He believed truth that said he could have the dream in his heart. He didn't beleive the lie that said, "You're secure with your regular paycheck. Don't take a chance on losing that and all your savings besides."

This man took the Word of God and used it to operate all of the affairs of his life. This man grabbed hold of the dream in his heart and the plan of God for his life. This man made the right choice.

When this man took the Bible—written truth—and got his thinking and decision-making in line with its laws and promises, it was easy for him to make the right choices and come into his complete success.

THE BATTLE OF TEMPTATION

The biggest battle you will ever wage to keep you from your success will be fought in your mind. Your mind is the battleground for choice—right or wrong.

Remember, it's the devil's job to come to you with lies just as he did to Adam and Eve in the Garden of Eden. The devil still brings his lies to steal, kill and destroy whom he can.

It is his job to steal your authority, your position in this life, and even your eternal life.

The devil comes to rob you of your heaven on earth. He comes to rob you of your prosperity...your health...your peace of mind...your success. He comes to fill you with fear and doubt so that you won't take hold of everything that God created you to have. The devil came to tempt you to make the wrong choices.

But Jesus—truth—came that you might have life and that life abundantly.

Jesus came so that you can see things as they really are—so that you can make the right choices.

YOU ARE THE DOORKEEPER OF YOUR MIND

The Bible tells us that lies and truth wage a battle in our minds, but that we are the "doorkeepers" of our own minds. We can allow things to enter our minds and we can keep other things out. We have that authority—that power of choice.

You are the one who must keep thoughts of...

"It's not really God's will for me to prosper"

"I'm sick and must learn to live with it"

"I just don't have the kind of personality he has, so it's no wonder I am not popular"

"I'm afraid to step out and take a chance"

"I just don't have what it takes to be successful"

...from entering your mind.

THE CHOICE IS YOURS

You must take your authority over doubt and unbelief and fear. *You* must choose those good things God wants to give you.

- Choose health
  - Choose prosperity
    - Choose heaven on earth
      - Choose abundant life
        - Choose success

The choice is yours. Make a decision to be everything that God created you to be.

Dare to exercise your power of choice. Make God's choice of success for your life YOUR CHOICE.

SUCCESS REVIEW:

- Whether you realize it or not, you have the power to choose to make your life a failure or a success.
- God gives us the choice between receiving His blessings or letting them go unclaimed.
- Ask God for what you want, or you're going to have to settle for what you get.
- The truth has come in the person of Jesus. The will of God as it is in heaven has come in Jesus to set us free from failure—free to receive success.
- You're not limited by your senses to the quality of life God has for you. You are only limited by your decision to make the wrong or right choice.

SUCCESS TRUTH:

Ideas are like seeds—they must be sown, cultivated, watered, pruned and developed, or they will not bear fruit.

5

DARE TO REALIZE YOUR DREAMS THROUGH THE POWER OF AN INSPIRED IDEA

It's really important for you to have a vision, a goal or a dream. Another way to say it is, "It's important for you to have an inspired idea."

There is a Bible verse that says it this way:

"Where there is no vision, the people perish..." (Proverbs 29:18).

You see, unless you have some goals, some dreams, a vision, you perish in your spirit. Your enthusiasm wanes. You lose your "get-up-and-go."

Another scripture says this:

"Hope deferred maketh the heart sick: but when the desire cometh, it is a tree of life" (Proverbs 13:12).

I think that half the sickness and disease in the world today—maybe even more than half—is a result of people not seeing their dreams come to pass. They gave up. They lost hope. They decided that they had no reason to live.

Think about many of the people who retire. They quit going to work, they don't take up substitute activities, and so their brains become inactive and their bodies become inactive. Soon the muscles in their bodies atrophy, they have no interest in life, they see no reason for living.

God wants you to have a dream!

God wants you to have a vision!

God wants you to have hope!

God wants the desires of your heart to become a reality!

God wants you to begin to see the good things He has planned and prepared for your life!

GOD WANTS TO GIVE YOU HIS INSPIRED IDEAS

Let me share some success stories with you which are examples of what can happen when you act on God's inspired ideas. These men didn't say, "Oh, that's ridiculous!" They chose instead to believe that great things can come from one tiny idea.

- There was a 40 year old man working for $20 a week. He had an inspired idea to mass-produce the automobile. Twenty years later he was the richest man in the world.
  HIS NAME WAS HENRY FORD.

- A man sitting on the front porch of his house, watching his cat claw at a canary in a cage, had an inspired idea. He saw a way to get cotton off a seed and invented the cotton gin.
  HIS NAME WAS ELI WHITNEY.

- A man whose talent was in knowing color and how to use it to make things beautiful had an inspired idea. He founded a cosmetics business that made him wealthy. It was the Revlon company.
  HIS NAME WAS CHARLES REVSON.

YOU CAN GET INSPIRED IDEAS TOO

Researchers say that over 2,000 ideas a day pass through our minds. All we need to do is capture that one good, sound inspired idea and act on it to see it become a reality.

WHAT IS AN IDEA?

The word idea is defined as ''to be wise, to see, to know a plan.''

The thing we need to be sure about is, ''Is this *my* idea based on my own feelings, or is it *God's idea* according to His plan of success for my life?''

The Bible verse that helped me answer this question is from Proverbs 16:3...

"Commit thy works unto the Lord, and thy thoughts shall be established."

This means that you must purpose in your heart to entrust God with *every* area of your life—your family, your marriage, your health, your work, everything. Choose to give His Word first place in your decisions. And (here's the promise that will be the result of your obedience) He will cause your thoughts to become agreeable to His will—then they shall succeed.

God will give you creative, inspired ideas, and if you act on them according to His plan, they shall successfully come to pass.

How do ideas come? They come in the form of a hunch. a strong thought that won't go away, intuition, a knowing that you know.

I believe God gives every one of us daily ideas so that we can make it successful through life. But, remember this:

Ideas are like seeds. They must be sowed, cultivated, watered, pruned, and developed, or they will not bear fruit.

There are seeds of greatness on the inside of you. A seed has potential energy inside of it. That's why there is so much power resident in an inspired idea.

People travel all over the world, spend most of their lives searching to find their place in life. And all the time the potential is living right on the inside of them waiting to be discovered and utilized.

I like what John D. Rockefeller said. *"A key to success is common people doing common things uncommonly."*

What he is saying is that anyone has the possibility of greatness, or success. I think my own life is an example of that.

I DARED TO BE A SUCCESS

Every good thing I have has come to me by the hand of God. Every success I have seen accomplished in my life is because I acted on my inspired ideas. Actually, I have so many ideas that I can't act on all of them, so I give some away and see others benefit from them too.

One day the idea for a whole satellite network came to me. It was innovative and exciting, so I followed God's plan through to the eventual success that we are now seeing. As of this writing, we have a network of over 1,900 affiliate churches across North America to whom we broadcast daily and monthly seminars which reach thousands and thousands of people. Eventually this satellite network will reach around the world.

Already about fifteen other similar networks have started because others saw the same potential in my one inspired idea. They say imitation is the highest form of flattery. I say that if God is the One who gives the idea, He means for it to grow and to benefit as many people as possible. What I am sharing with you in this book can also be shared with thousands, maybe millions of people, via the medium of television because I acted on an inspired idea and saw it come to pass.

I knew nothing about satellites or receiver dishes when I got this inspired idea. But with it came an element of excitement. I didn't have the money to carry it out either. But I knew that I didn't have to concern myself with money. You get a good idea, and the idea will produce the money.

A SUCCESS STORY

Let me give you another example of this.

Years ago there was a minister who had an inspired idea. His name was Frank Gonzales, and his idea was to build a trade school for those who could not afford to go to another school. He knew he didn't have the money to see his dream come to pass, but he became consumed by this idea.

He knew that this school was going to cost about one million dollars to build, and he didn't have one million dollars. All he had was about 100 people who came to his church. So he decided to run an ad in the paper announcing that his Sunday message would be titled, ''What I would do if I had a million dollars.''

The following Sunday, the church was packed. Everyone wanted to find out what Pastor Frank would do if he had a million dollars. That morning he preached his message with his whole heart. He shared with the congregation the burden he had to see young people have an opportunity to learn a trade and be able to do things with their lives they couldn't afford to do otherwise.

At the end of the service an older man stood up and walked toward him.

''Pastor, Monday morning I will have a check for you for one million dollars.''

That man was Frank D. Armour from the Armour meat packing firm.

Today that school is the Illinois Institute of Technology. It is a school that has trained thousands of students.

Because of one man's inspired idea—because he dared to be a success—countless numbers of people were able to benefit from his success.

WHAT ABOUT YOU?

- What would you do if you had a million dollars?
- What dream would you dream?
- How many benefits can you count from just that one dream?
- How many people would your one dream touch?

REAL WISDOM TAPS THE
UNTAPPED POTENTIAL

Real wisdom is the ability to see beyond what is around you. Real wisdom captures the untapped potential of the seeds of inspired ideas, those seeds which are with you waiting to be cultivated and harvested.

Too many times we have such wonderful inspired ideas and we don't act on them, and we miss the very thing God is trying to accomplish for us and for others.

You can't be a little thinker and expect God to give you big ideas.

You have to think big. Then God will give you some big ideas.

STIMULATING STEPS

Here are some steps you can take which will stimulate your mind to receive and recognize inspired ideas.

1. Look beyond what you see around you.
2. Renew your mind with "God's Success Manual"—The Bible.
3. Commit all areas of your life to God.
4. Ask God to reveal His wisdom to you.
5. Expect God to give you inspired ideas.

And once you begin to receive what may be inspired ideas, here are some pointers to help you judge them.

1. Write your ideas down.
2. Ask yourself if they line up with God's Word.
3. Consider all the possible benefits of the idea.
4. Think about what must transpire to bring your idea to pass.
5. If the idea is inspired by God, He will show you what steps to take.

Your idea may be just a little nugget of gold. Be alert. It may be the nugget that leads to the mother load!

I have found that most ideas are the tip of the iceberg. So don't float by the iceberg just because you can only see the tip.

Possibly you have been sitting back waiting for God to move.

He has already moved! Now He's waiting for *you* to move! He has given *you* the power to realize your dreams. How? Through the power of an inspired idea.

Now all you have to do is act on what is already yours, and it will revolutionize your life.

SUCCESS REVIEW:

...Real wisdom is the ability to see beyond what is around you.

...You can't be a *little* thinker and expect *big* ideas.

...God will give you inspired ideas and, if you act on them according to His plan, they shall succeed.

...You don't have to concern yourself with money. Get a good idea and the idea will produce the money.

SUCCESS TRUTH:

Unless your mental actions are followed by physical actions, the total plan of success for your life cannot be fully accomplished.

6

DARE TO STEP INTO THE POWER OF ACTION

You can desire success. You can see things as they really are. You can harness your mind with the truth of God's Word. You can choose to pursue God's plan for your life. You can recognize that many of the ideas which you get are inspired by God for your success.

But these are just acts of your will—results of mental actions.

Unless your mental actions are followed by physical actions, the total plan of success for your life cannot be fully accomplished.

Even if you say the right words, it isn't enough. I know some people who for years only *talk* about their big dreams. All they *ever* do is talk. They never actually *do* anything. They never take the actions which would accomplish their big plans and make their dreams come true. They talk about what they can do, but they never really *do* it! The only energy they exert is hot air!

Sure, words are important, but without the power of action behind them, they will remain mere words. Nothing will really come to pass.

CLIMBING YOUR SUCCESS MOUNTAIN

By taking one step at a time, you can begin to be a success through the power of action.

It's the same way in mountain-climbing. You get to the top only by taking one step at a time—by putting one foot in front of the other and moving forward. Sometimes you have to grasp the steep sides of the mountain with your hands and pull yourself up. But every exertion that takes you to the top is in the physical realm.

Sure, you preceded your mountain-climbing with careful plans and mental conditioning, but you still get to the top by taking that one step at a time.

Many people think that if they can't jump to the top of the mountain right away they're not even going to try. So they never even take that first step. That's how procrastination and inaction will rob you of your ultimate success.

And some people think that if they can't do it perfectly they won't do it at all. So they never even start. But I suggest thinking about the old saying: *"If it's worth doing, it's worth doing imperfectly...until you can do it perfectly!"*

A PERFECT EXAMPLE

I can give you a perfect example of what I am trying to say from my own life.

My wife Marte and I had just started out in the ministry and were living in Houston. We had no money and were existing on beans and cornbread. I was trying to be obedient to God, but still the situation looked disastrous.

I remember that we had been out of money for several days, had no gasoline, and soon would have no more food.

We lived in a little travel trailer we had parked in a parking lot—not even a trailer park. Roaches lived with us fighting for the remaining crumbs of food. It looked like the end of our world.

Marte began to say we should have never gone into the ministry. If I looked at what I saw with my eyes, I would have had to agree with her. But I knew I was following God's plan for my life, so I had to depend upon Him for an inspired idea that would provide for my family. I really got serious with God.

"Father, I have given my life to You. I followed your plan for my life and went into the ministry. I am preaching and teaching, just as You led me to do. Now I know that You promise in Your Word that you will supply all of our needs, if we are being obedient. I don't know what else I can do. You just have to tell me. You have to give me your wisdom...your inspired idea.''

I didn't want to go on a welfare line. I didn't want to beg family or friends for a handout. I wanted to go right to the Source of my supply—God Himself. Sure, He could use people to give me money, but *He* was going to have to ask them—*not me.*

Sure enough, the very next morning as I woke up, God spoke His inspired idea through my thoughts. I knew that it was Him. He said only the words, ''Paul had a tent-making job,'' and I knew just what He meant.

Paul was a preacher and teacher too. He is recorded in the New Testament as a disciple of Jesus who supported his ministry largely with his tentmaking profession.

I was to continue working in a trade until my ministry was self-supporting. That is what God was telling me.

The next thought I had was another inspired idea: I was to pursue the town's popular cedar fence trade. I just knew this was God's direction for me. So I put some action behind the idea and went to a fence company.

I told the boss I was the world's greatest fence builder.

''You ever built a fence before?'' he asked.

''No,'' I answered, ''but I've watched them do it, and if *they* can do it, *I* can do it!''

I bugged the guy. I insisted. I projected all the confidence I could muster. And I convinced him.

''O.K. I'll give you a try. Here's a load of pickets. Here's the address. Go build the fence, and I'll come look at it. If I like your work, you're hired.''

Marte and I had a hammer, a screwdriver, a drill, and a power saw. Even though I had it, I had never used the saw before in my life. But I was determined to build the best fence the town of Houston had ever seen!

Somehow, we were able to get the fence up. The boss came to look at it. We didn't have to rebuild too much of it, so he said we could build some more. I had a job! With Marte's help, I was now a professional fence-builder as well as a preacher.

God had supplied the inspired idea, but *I* had to institute the appropriate action for the idea to bear fruit. I could see the fence in my mind; I could see the boss giving me my paycheck; I could even tell him how terrific my fence-building techniques and abilities were...BUT until I put forth the effort to actually build the fence, I wouldn't benefit from it in any way.

Are you getting the point? Maybe this will help.

DIRECTION FOR YOUR DREAMS

I can also equate the power of action with the launching of a rocket.

The sophisticated computerized guidance system—the specialized technical radar equipment—doesn't totally operate until *after* the rocket has left the launching pad.

It's like that with you. Once you take a step of action—once you begin to do something—then God will give you direction for your dreams, and you will find success. Your action activates His power to work on your behalf!

WHAT THE BIBLE SAYS ABOUT ACTION

James 2:14 in the Weymouth version of the Bible has this to say about action:

"What good is it, my brethren, if a man professes to have faith, and yet his actions do not correspond?"

In other words, a person's faith (or his belief in the value of his dream or goal) has to cooperate with his actions. Actions bring about the evidence of your faith. Actions prove your unseen faith with results which are visable.

ANOTHER EXAMPLE

I can provide you with another example from my own experience. Actually, I have hundreds, maybe thousands, of personal examples. This one should give you the idea.

In the early days of our ministry, I had another inspired idea. This time it was an idea for Christian greeting cards—an idea which at the time was for a unique design.

I drew the pictures, and Marte came up with the appropriate words and Bible verses.

We bought the paper at a discount price and brought them to a printer.

We brought the cards to different Christian bookstores. Each store would buy only six or seven cards at a time. In figuring out our expenses—gas money to get to the stores, paper, envelopes, and printing costs—it didn't take me long to see that I wasn't making any profit this way. I needed an inspired idea that would give my dream more direction.

I turned to God once more and reminded Him of two of His promises from the Bible:

1. *"Call unto me, and I will answer thee, and shew thee great and mighty things, which thou knowest not"* (Jeremiah 33:3).

2. *"...Ask me of things to come concerning my sons, and concerning the work of my hands command ye me"* (Isaiah 45:11).

I remember that I was driving down the freeway when I "saw" the inspired solution. I "saw" those greeting cards of ours in a little cedar shadow box. The box held 70 cards.

I turned to Marte with a shout, "I've got it! I know what we can do to make a profit. Since they'll buy seven cards, we know they like them. So why can't we expect them to buy 70 instead of 7, if they're packaged properly. We'll sell them by the rack."

So we bought some cedar and cut and nailed it to form two-by-one-foot size boxes.

We went behind furniture stores and got those big cardboard mattress boxes to put on the back of the wood boxes.

Then we folded the cards and stuffed the envelopes by hand. We wrapped each package with plastic and sealed it with a soldering iron, and we used a hairdryer to shrink-wrap the plastic. God showed us how to do it all, saving money with each step. It was primitive, but it was profitable!

Every store we went to with these new racks bought one! We were selling 90% of our greeting cards that way. The rest we sold individually at meetings where we spoke and ministered. With this new sales method we sometimes made as much as $200 a day in income.

This was all because of an idea...and then *acting* on that idea.

SUCCESS ACTION STEPS

I believe it will help to give you some definite action steps that will ''give feet to your faith.''

1. Write down your inspired idea.

2. Write your plan of action on the same sheet.

3. When you are sure of what you are going to do, put words behind your idea and tell the people who need to be involved in helping you carry it out.

4. Put action behind your words and do what you need to do to see your dream become a reality.

I want you to make a decision today that you are going to begin to go forward...that you are going to ''give feet to your faith''...and let your actions speak louder than words.

Right now I dare you to step into the power of action so that you can see God's plan of success for your life come into being.

SUCCESS REVIEW:

- Unless your *mental* actions are followed by *physical* actions, the total plan of success for your life cannot be fully accomplished.
- Your action activates God's power to work on your behalf.
- Actions prove your *unseen* faith with results which are *visible.*

SUCCESS TRUTH:

Since God is the source of your power to get wealth, then without the help of God, no one can be wealthy.

7

DARE TO ACTIVATE YOUR POWER TO CREATE WEALTH

I can tell you assuredly that God does want you to prosper and that it is God who gives you the power to create wealth.

How can I be so sure of that?

Because I have taken it right from the Bible—God's own "Success Manual." Let me show you.

> "But thou shalt remember the Lord thy God: for it is He that giveth thee power to get wealth, that He may establish His covenant which He sware unto thy fathers, as it is this day" (Deuteronomy 8:18).

I want to point out three things to you from this verse. It is important for you to understand this verse because it contains God's principles concerning prosperity that can put you on the road to your success.

1. Don't forget God. Remember Him.
2. God is your Source of supply.
3. God's promise (covenant) is that you will be blessed so that you can bless others.

Since God is the source of your power to get wealth, then without the help of God, no one can be wealthy.

You can gain all the world's riches, but without giving God first place in your life, you will not enjoy them.

YOU CAN HAVE WHAT YOU WANT

Now if you don't believe that you are supposed to be prosperous or have the good things of this life, then guess what? You won't get very much. Why?

You have to be the one who desires to get out from under the influence of lack. God won't force you to take the good things which can be yours. Remember that we learned that as you think in your heart, so are you? Well, then if you *think* lack, you will *have* lack. If you think lack, that's the way you will be.

WHY SETTLE FOR SECOND BEST?

But God, who only wants the best for those who love Him, says that He has given us the power to get wealth. In the original Hebrew this means:

- To make wealth
- To bring forth wealth
- To procure wealth
- To bring wealth into being
- To design or invent something
- To call forth something to happen
- To create wealth

A good idea—an inspired idea—has the power to create wealth. Why? Because when an idea is sown, like a seed it can reap a harvest. Let me give you some real-life examples of this about people whose names you may recognize.

SUCCESS STORIES

- This young man was raised by a Christian mother who taught him that 10% of everything that he earned belonged to God. So when he

began to work at the age of 16, he gave 10% of his earnings away to God's work. By the time he was 33 he was a millionaire. By the age of 43 he had the largest company in the world. Sadly, when he was 53 something happened and he stopped giving God first place in his life. It was then that he got a horrible disease, and the doctors told him he would die before he was 54 years old. The man repented, turned back to God, and he lived to be 98 years old, giving many millions of dollars away, just as he had before. And the foundations he established are still giving away millions long after his death.

HIS NAME WAS JOHN D. ROCKEFELLER

- Another man was struggling through life and didn't think he was going to make it. He turned to a minister for advice and was told, "Son, you need to make God your Senior Partner in business, and He will give you the success you are seeking." The man did what the minister advised and became one of the largest manufacturers of cheese in the world.
HIS NAME WAS J. L. KRAFT

- This man had a love for the hotel business. He had three small hotels—one in San Antonio, one in El Paso, and one in Wichita Falls. When the Great Depression hit the country, he lost them all. But he was a praying man. Even though he was broke and in debt, he knew that God would not fail him. And he held on to his dream of the hotel business and even of owning the majestic Waldorf Astoria Hotel in New York City. He maintained his principles of prayer, faith and hard work, and God moved on his behalf. He got back his hotels through a miracle and, yes, fifteen years later he not only owned those but the great Waldorf Astoria as well. He was the first to open a chain of international hotels, becoming the owner of the most hotels in the world.
HIS NAME WAS CONRAD HILTON

All of these men represent this fact: God's success principles will work for you if you will work for them. And, if you will do the sowing, God will do the growing.

YOU WERE MADE FOR PROSPERITY TOO

God wants you to prosper just as much as He wanted these famous men to prosper—in *every* area of your life:

"Beloved, I wish above all things that thou mayest prosper [that's His desire for you financially] *and be in health* [that's His desire for you physically and emotionally], *even as thy soul prospereth* [that's His desire for you spiritually]" (III John 2).

This Bible verse makes it very clear that God wants you to prosper in the three areas of your life that cover *all* the areas of your life:

- Financial (have all your needs met)
- Physical and emotional (have health)
- Spiritual (have a relationship with God)

You see, God is not opposed to you having money and the good things of life, or He would not have given you the power to create wealth. *He is not opposed to you having things; He just doesn't want things to have you!* He is not opposed to you having money because money is not the root of all evil, as you have heard. No, it's the LOVE of money that is the root of all evil.

God wants first place in your heart, not money, and when you put God first, the prosperity in *all* areas will naturally follow.

WHAT IS TRUE WEALTH?

Here is something else you need to know to put all of this in its proper perspective: True wealth is not merely money. Money is just the outward appearance of wealth. True wealth is not on the outward. True wealth is what you know—your level of wisdom on the inward.

Remember, the definition of the words ''wisdom,'' or ''wise,'' in the simplest form is, ''the ability to see.''

Let me give you an example. I shared with you that at the age of forty, Henry Ford was making twenty dollars a week. But then he got the idea to mass-produce automobiles, and by the time he was sixty, he was the richest man in the world.

Well, someone came to him one day and said, ''Mr. Ford, what would happen if you lost all of your money and all of your possessions?''

His answer was wise. ''Sir, my wealth is not in material possessions; my wealth is in the information that I know, and the information that I know how to get my hands on.

''If everything was taken away from me and I had no more material possessions or financial wealth, because of what I know I would have the money and possessions back in less than five years.''

You see what I am trying to show you? You get a good idea, and the idea will produce the money! If you have wisdom operating in your life, it is more precious than gold. Because, as Ford knew, you can lose gold in a minute, but you can never lose your wisdom—the things that you know—because they are buried deep inside of you. And it is that wisdom which really produces the money.

FOUR WAYS TO GET MONEY

There are four ways you can go after money in this life:

1. Borrow it.
2. Beg for it.
3. Steal it.
4. Earn it.

The word ''earn'' is defined as ''to introduce something new into existence and to harvest the yield that it produces.'' It's when you go to work eight hours a day, forty hours a week, then you harvest a paycheck for your time and labor. It is God's law of sowing and reaping in operation.

But the welfare system gives a man his food and money without his having to work for it, while God's way is through developing His wisdom in your life so that you will always have the ability to earn money...even if the government system fails.

WORLD'S BEST SERMON

There was a minister named Russell Conwell who years ago preached what many consider the world's greatest sermon. It has been preached more times than any other message. It has been duplicated on tapes, written in books, and read by people all over the world. It was so good that even those who didn't believe in God discovered and used it for the wisdom it contained.

The title is "Acres of Diamonds," and the message is this:

A man had a farm, but it wasn't enough. He wanted to be rich. He wanted to find great wealth. So he sold his farm to travel around the world in his quest for the great treasure he desired.

In the meantime, the man who bought the farm was out by the creek one day. He happened to look down just as the sun caught something sparkling on the ground. He picked it up to discover that it was a beautiful diamond.

That one diamond turned out to be one of the most valuable diamonds ever discovered. And the farm became the world's most famous diamond mine.

The original owner was traveling all over the world to find his riches, but they were in his own backyard all the time—he just didn't know it.

People travel all over the world to find their place and purpose in life and to capture success. But all along it is right inside of them like a seed, waiting to be cultivated!

FROM A SEED TO A GREAT HARVEST

In 1976 when Marte and I came to settle in Dallas, after being called into the ministry and preaching in other cities, we had $300 in our pockets. Now, only 10 years later, our building and about 25 acres of our land along a major Dallas freeway have been appraised at a value of about 18 million dollars! How did we do it?

Marte and I tapped into the principles of success—one of which is that God gives you the power and the inner abilities to create wealth.

WHAT ARE THE KEYS TO SUCCESS?

Let's go over those success principles one more time so that you can really understand them, see them as a whole picture, and get them into your heart so they will become a way of life. As you read them, say them out loud as a verbal expression of your commitment to put these principles to work on your behalf.

1. Commit yourself to reaching your maximum potential through God's plan for your life.
2. Commit yourself to learning and living by God's Source Book of Truth—The Bible.
3. Commit yourself to guarding your mind—reject lies and receive truth.
4. Commit yourself to pursuing the dream in your heart by the direction of inspired ideas.
5. Commit yourself to the necessary actions that will fulfill God's success plan for your life.
6. Commit yourself to God so that you may receive the true wealth of inner riches.

I would have to say that the last step is the most important, for without taking that one last step, the others would not really have power or true meaning. You see, the last step should really be the first one.

So, to give power to your success plan, read on into the next chapter and carry out God's plan of success for your life to the very fullest.

Right now...today...I challenge you to be all that you were created to be. I DARE YOU TO BE A SUCCESS...A SUCCESS IN LIFE THROUGH THE LORDSHIP OF JESUS CHRIST!

SUCCESS REVIEW:

- God is not opposed to you having things; He just doesn't want things to have you.
- True wealth is not merely money; true wealth is your inward level of wisdom.
- God's success principles will work for you if you will work for them. If you do the sowing, God will do the growing.
- Commit yourself to God so that you may be able to receive the true wealth of inner riches.

SUCCESS TRUTH:
"I (Jesus) came that they may have and enjoy life, and have it in abundance—to the full, till it overflows."
John 10:10 (AMP)

8

DARE TO BEGIN
YOUR NEW LIFE

All that I have shared with you in this book up to now is just the beginning of what I teach on success in life. But, along with what is contained in this chapter, it is enough to revolutionize your life.

I have challenged you to launch out and DARE TO BE A SUCCESS because I know success is God's plan for your life. I don't want you to miss *any part* of His plan because it is through that entire plan that you will reach your maximum potential and find your true success.

In order to understand how important the final step toward your success really is, I want to share a true story with you. It is the story of an eagle.

It seems the eagle was kept as a pet for ten years, confined to the limitations of life in a cage. One day his owner decided to set him free. The sky was his true realm. There would be no limits there, living where he was really created to live.

When the eagle was placed outside of his cage, it was a cloudy day, and he just stood there.

Would he fly? Would he be unable to? He hadn't flown for ten years. He wasn't familiar with the real world outside of his cage.

As the eagle stood there looking around, the clouds parted and the sun came out. A ray of sunlight hit right where that eagle was standing.

When he saw the light, it was as if it sparked new life in him. He opened up his wings...he flapped them in place for a moment...and then suddenly he was airborne. He was free! He had somehow received the power to operate in a new world—a world he had never known before. He had dared to begin a new life!

DARE TO BEGIN *YOUR* NEW LIFE

Some of you who are reading this have also been living a limited life—a life without meaning and power. Some of you don't know that there is a whole new world for you to enter.

It's time for the "light" to hit you too.

It's time for you to stretch your "wings" and fly.

It's time to be everything you were created to be.

IT'S TIME TO DARE TO BEGIN YOUR NEW LIFE!

HOW TO BE BORN AGAIN

You don't have to clean up your life before you can be born again. God will clean up your life. Asking Jesus Christ to cleanse you of your sins is more than a request for forgiveness. It causes a supernatural event to happen. God gives you a new heart, new desires, and the spirit of truth. Following those new desires, which are based on God's Word, will give you a beautiful new life on earth, and an eternal life in God's Kingdom.

Why should I read this?

"So then faith cometh by hearing, and hearing by the word of God" (Romans 10:17).

Who is Jesus, and why do I need Him?

"He was in the world, and though the world was made through him, the world did not recognize him...Yet to all who received him, to those who believed in his name, he gave the right to become children of God, children born not of natural descent, nor of human decision or a husband's will, but born of God" (John 1:10-13 NIV).

"Whoever believes in the Son has eternal life, but whoever rejects the Son will not see life, for God's wrath remains on him" (John 3:36 NIV).

"For God so loved the world, that he gave his only begotten Son, that whosoever believeth in him should not perish, but have everlasting life" (John 3:16).

"I am the way and the truth and the life. No one comes to the Father except through me" (John 14:6 NIV).

Why did Jesus die for me?

"This righteousness from God comes through faith in Jesus Christ to all who believe. There is no difference, for all have sinned and fall short of the glory of God, and are justified freely by his grace through the redemption that came by Jesus Christ. God presented him as a sacrifice of atonement, through faith in his blood. He did this to demonstrate his justice, because in his forbearance he had left the sins committed beforehand unpunished—he did it to demonstrate his justice at the present time, so as to be just and the one who justifies the man who has faith in Jesus" (Romans 3:22-26 NIV).

Am I a sinner even if I believe in God and Jesus?

"I tell you the truth, unless a man is born again, he cannot see the kingdom of God" (John 3:3 NIV).

"If God were your Father, you would love me, for I came from God and now am here" (John 8:42 NIV).

"If ye love me, keep my commandments" (John 14:15).

How do I get saved from my sins?

"If we confess our sins, he is faithful and just to forgive us our sins, and to cleanse us from all unrighteousness" (I John 1:9).

"If thou shalt confess with thy mouth the Lord Jesus, and shalt believe in thine heart that God hath raised him from the dead, thou shalt be saved" (Romans 10:9).

Is that all? I don't have to DO anything?

"For by grace are ye saved through faith; and that not of yourselves: it is the gift of God: Not of works, lest any man should boast" (Ephesians 1:8-9).

"Therefore, there is now no condemnation for those who are in Christ Jesus, because through Christ Jesus the law of the Spirit of life set me free from the law of sin and death" (Romans 8:1 NIV).

Do I have to change now?

NO! Let God change you! Give Him your life. He'll give you a new heart. You are now a new creature.

"Therefore if any man be in Christ, he is a new creature: old things are passed away; behold, all things are become new" (II Corinthians 5:17).

Be born again. Grow spiritually by feeding on the Word of God—the Bible. Talk (pray) to your heavenly Father in the name of Jesus. Commit yourself to a body of believers—a church. Determine now to believe God's Word and His promises above all circumstances in this life.

PRAY THIS PRAYER AND BELIEVE:

Father in heaven, I've heard Your Word, and I want to be born again. Jesus, cleanse me of my sins. I want to be a child of God. I want to give my life to You. Make me a new person. Be my Lord and Savior.

I believe I'm now born again because, God, Your Word says I am. Jesus is my Lord. Thank You, Jesus, for a new life. Amen.

Now, don't go by what you think or feel. Go by what God's Word says. You are saved! Believe it!

Now, go ahead and fly. Go ahead and DARE TO BE A SUCCESS!

ABOUT THE AUTHOR

Dr. Robert G. Tilton, founder and pastor of the 8,000 member Word of Faith World Outreach Center in Dallas, Texas and host of *Success·N·Life,* a daily television and radio Christian talk show, has come to a vital understanding that God desires His people to be achievers in this lifetime.

But he has not always been such a prosperous individual. Born in 1946, and raised a Baptist in rural Texas, he grew up amidst struggle, dilemma and discouragement.

Drifting far from his religious roots, twenty-two-year-old Robert Tilton married lovely Marte Phillips, and later shifted from a comfortable role in the engineering field to become a successful home designer and builder. After embracing a lifestyle which resulted in a plethora of problems, the worldly entrepreneur encountered young street evangelists who introduced him to the Lord Jesus Christ, and he soon learned to follow God with his whole heart. Later struggling as a tent evangelist, he came to seek God's better way and to learn His Kingdom principles.

In 1976 God spoke to Robert Tilton: ''Go to Farmers Branch, Texas, and build a family church and full gospel training center.'' That church, now a Dallas landmark, encompasses a wide variety of ministries, including a Leadership and Bible Institute, a Christian academy, a monthly satellite seminar broadcast, a publications company, and the 24-hour Success·N·Life Satellite Network.

Dr. Tilton has been acknowledged as one of the outstanding Christian communicators of the times, and is eagerly welcomed in assemblies nationwide as a teacher and speaker expounding on God's success principles. You cannot hear Robert Tilton without making a decision, because he challenges you to be all that God created you to be.